CELEBRITY READERS

Famous Female Sports Stars

REM 477

A TEACHING RESOURCE FROM...

REMEDIA
PUBLICATIONS

BLACKLINE
MASTERS

AUTHORS
Joan Stringham
Mary Keller

COVER ART
Danny Beck

To find Remedia products in a store near you, visit:
http://www.rempub.com/stores

REMEDIA PUBLICATIONS, INC.
15887 N. 76TH STREET • SUITE 120 • SCOTTSDALE, AZ • 85260

477

Name _____

Across

1. She is also an _____.
3. The Olympic _____ was passed from runner to runner.
4. Her stepdad was the first to notice she had _____ as a runner.
6. The 2000 _____ opened in Australia.
8. Even before that win, she was a national _____.
10. She lit the _____ that would burn throughout the games.
11. Thanks to Freeman, many children have now learned that they can _____.

Down

1. Cathy is an _____.
2. She _____.
5. Her _____ was the first to see that she had talent.
7. She _____ to the gold medal in the 400-meters in 2000.
9. The Aborigines were there before the _____ people came.

Research: Use a dictionary. Find **billabong**. Write the definition. From what country does the word come?

CYNTHIA **COOPER**

The Blossoming of a Late Bloomer

Cynthia Cooper begged the high school coach to teach her about basketball. At first, he refused. She persisted. Finally, he gave in. He taught her to dribble the ball with her left hand and with her right hand. She learned how to shoot hoops. Many children get started in their sports by the time they are eight or nine. At 16, Cynthia was a "late bloomer."

Cooper lived in Watts in Los Angeles. The neighborhood was tough. Her mother worked hard to support her eight children.

Cynthia had a poor sense of self worth as a child. When she got into basketball, that changed. She found out she was more than a good athlete. She was great. In her senior year, she was one of the best high school players. She could score 45 points a game.

There was no pro women's basketball league in the U.S. in 1986. Cooper went to Europe and played in Italy and Spain. She spent 11 years there. She was the best player on the European circuit. Eight times, Cynthia led the league in scoring. "Coop" became known as the best female basketball player in the world.

In 1997, the Women's National Basketball Association was started. Teams formed around the U.S. Cynthia joined the Houston Comets. Four years in a row, the Comets won the national championships. In 2000, Cooper retired. She had won the Most Valuable Player award every year she was in the WNBA. She was clearly a leader in women's basketball.

Answer the questions.

1. Who taught Cynthia about basketball? _____

2. How old was Cooper when she learned to play basketball? _____

3. What do you think it means to be a "late bloomer"? _____

   _____

   _____

   _____

4. In what city did Cynthia live? _____

5. In her senior year, how many points could she score in a game? _____

   _____

6. In what two countries in Europe did "Coop" play? _____

   _____

7. What did her team win four years in a row?_____

   _____

8. In what year was the WNBA started? _____

9. What team did Cynthia join? _____

10. In what sport was she a leader? _____

11. What award did she win every year? _____

    _____

Research: Use a dictionary. Find **professional** and **amateur**. What is the main difference between the two?

BRANDI **CHASTAIN**

A Voice for Soccer

"She's always wanted to be the voice of the sport," soccer coach DiCicco said. "She just needed that one kick to give her the license to do it." That kick was the winning point for the World Cup in 1999. Brandi and her U.S. teammates made history that day.

Brandi was born in California in 1968. The first time she wore a soccer uniform, she was eight years old. She loved it. A week went by before her mom could talk her into taking off the uniform. Soccer became a passion for her. The Olympic Development Program took an interest in her when she was 12. The talented girl was on her way to being a star athlete. She played for her college team. Brandi led them to the playoffs. The team was ranked third in the nation.

Chastain played for the U.S. team in the 1996 Olympics. Brandi's knee was hurt during the semifinals. There were five matches left. She played every minute of every match. The U.S. won the gold. Winning the

Olympics and the World Cup gave women's sports a big boost.

In 2000, Chastain and the U.S. team competed in Australia for the gold medal. The game went into overtime. The score was tied at 2-2. The Norwegian team kicked the goal to win the gold medal. The Americans won the silver.

Brandi said, "We're very, very proud of what we have accomplished. And I hope everybody who watches the game understands it wasn't easy."

Name _____

If the statement is a fact, circle the letter under FACT. If the statement is an opinion, circle the letter under OPINION.

	FACT	OPINION
1. Brandi is the best soccer player in the world.	N	M
2. Brandi was born in California in 1968.	E	A
3. Soccer became a passion for her.	X	C
4. Brandi would be even better at playing hockey.	Z	I
5. She is not very nice.	H	C
6. In the 2000 Olympics, the U.S. team lost to Norway.	A	E
7. Women's soccer is not as interesting as men's soccer.	L	N

What is one of Brandi's favorite types of food?

(Write the letters you have circled on the lines.)

____ ____ ____ ____ ____ ____ ____

Write your opinion of the following statement:

Women should be allowed to play on men's soccer teams.

_____

_____

_____

Research: Use an encyclopedia. Find **Pelé**. What sport did he play? Where was he born? What year? For what U.S. team did he play in 1975? Why do you think this helped soccer to become popular in the U.S.?

Name _____

"Annamania"

By her mid teens, Anna Kournikova was already rich and famous. Her picture has been seen on the covers of magazines. Many people think she is quite beautiful. People are interested in what Anna does on and off the tennis courts.

Anna was born in 1981 in Moscow, Russia. At five, she received a special gift. "I found my first rackets under the Christmas tree," Anna said, "but I found out later that my parents sold one of their TV's to get me those rackets." By eight, it was clear that she was going to be a great tennis player. She and her mother moved to Florida. Anna attended a famous tennis school.

In 1995, she started playing junior tennis. At the end of her first season, she was named Junior World Champion. At 14, Anna turned pro. In 1996, she began her first full season with the WTA. She won the WTA's Newcomer of the Year award. Anna put the tennis world into a spin. It was the start of "Annamania."

When she shows up at a match, heads turn. She has created a huge following. People want to know what Anna wore. How did Anna fix her long, blond hair? Photos of her have been in newspapers around the world. In spite of the frenzy, Anna must focus on her game.

Of all the attention, Anna said, "For me, it's okay. I just try to go out there and play."

Name _____

Find the words in the box in the word search puzzle.

```
B A F Z U Q B L J O P U B M B V F D S D R
E E S R U S S I A F H J K R I C H I A Y V
A H K L Q L H R A Z S Q W M K H A F A B H
U M R U K H G F S W Q A R Z X D F G U D K
T S A T H E U N T N E W C O M E R D T N L
I O C I S H E D S I F O C U S J K I N J F
F D K N F I K H G B F Q K Z D B K F X M L
U M E E T F V F Y J K U E U H J U I M J O
L J T W C F A M O U S L T A X R J L L F R
T V S S D G J K U N T T S Y U K L B T K I
R D N P K G R A S T E N N I S R D F G E D
Z J H A R C J M B Q Z Q S V A X E H K K A
L D H P G T U K J G X M C N L V T J G N Z
O N R E J M N W I H F D S C F D C V M D G
H R L R J I I D O G H O N E D O C Y U Q M
U F R S U E O U C N D M R X D R U J U G O
J A C E G I R M J Y T I E M C D E D I V S
S A N V R J R S J T K S F R E N Z Y S N C
A C H R I S T M A S A X B J I S L M H S O
F E T X I D U B T F N F G Y H T W X H F W
A N N A M A N I A C D N J K A D T R U D A
```

focus	Moscow	Russia
Newcomer	rackets	famous
tennis	Florida	Junior
frenzy	newspapers	rich
beautiful	Christmas	Annamania

Research: In 1980, the U.S. boycotted the Olympics in Moscow. Use a dictionary. Find **boycott**. Write the definition.

TARA **LIPINSKI**

Skating with All Her Heart

Tara was born in 1982 in Philadelphia. She started roller-skating when she was three years old. Soon, she was doing turns and jumps on her skates. At five, she won a regional contest. Her mother and father let Tara try ice skating when she was six. Tara struggled to get her balance on the ice. Her folks did not want to make her nervous by watching, so they went to get some hot chocolate. They returned a few minutes later. Her mom and dad were surprised by what they saw. "She was doing jumps and turns on the ice," her mother said.

Tara worked hard at her skating. Sometimes she got up at 3:00 a.m. to attend lessons. At 12, she won first place at a major ice skating event. It had been only six years since her first lesson. Tara won a national title at 13. At 14, she won a gold medal at the World Championships.

Tiny Tara Lipinski skated a near-perfect program in the 1998

Olympics. She dazzled the crowd with her turns, spins, and leaps. She was 15. Tara said, "I took my position on the ice. Everything was flowing. I skated with all my heart. I soared through my jumps and danced through my footwork. I let my excitement show on my face and in the way I moved. When my scores came up, I let out a shout. I'd won! I had just become the youngest Winter Olympic gold medalist in history!"

Name _____

If the statement is true, circle the letter under TRUE. If the statement is false, circle the letter under FALSE.

	TRUE	FALSE
1. Tara started skateboarding when she was three.	R	F
2. She was born in Philadelphia.	R	G
3. Tara won a regional contest at five.	O	A
4. She started ice skating when she was six.	G	P
5. Tara never struggled on the ice.	M	S
6. Tara won a national title at 11.	I	A
7. Tara is good at ice hockey.	A	N
8. She won the World Championship at 14.	D	I
9. Tara was 16 when she skated in the 1998 Olympics.	E	D
10. Tara skated with all her heart.	O	D
11. Tara got up at 2 a.m. to attend lessons.	N	G
12. Tara was born in 1982.	S	Z

Write the letters you have circled above on the lines. You will learn what Tara's favorite animals are.

___ ___ ___ ___ ___   ___ ___ ___   ___ ___ ___ ___

Complete the sentences.

"I let my _____ show on my face and in the way I

_____. I had just become the _____

Winter Olympic _____ medalist in _____!"

Research: Use an encyclopedia. Find **Sonja Henie**. Where was she born? When was she born? What was her sport? What title did she win at age 10?

ALISON **SYDOR**

The Pride of Canada

Alison Sydor took to cycling as a little girl. Her family tells the story of her first bicycle ride. She was either two years old or three years old. It depends on who is telling the story. The stories agree on one thing. She rode the bicycle without any training.

As an adult, Sydor won world championships. She also won a silver medal at the 1996 Olympics in Atlanta. In the beginning, she was a road racer. There was no future for her professionally in road racing. She switched to mountain biking.

Alison lives in Victoria, British Columbia. After winning the silver medal, she began training hard for the 2000 Olympics in Australia. She had a good chance to win the gold medal in the cross-country race.

Three weeks before the games, Sydor caught a bad cold. She arrived in Sydney feeling ill. Training was intense. The day of the race, Alison was not at her peak. It was a disappointing day. In the first lap of the race, her chain broke. In the third lap, she crashed. After getting back on track, she was attacked by magpies. In spite of everything, she was still in the race. She finished fifth. She was just two minutes and 54 seconds behind the gold medal winner. "I wasn't far out of it. I just couldn't catch them today," she said.

Alison knew it was just one race. She said she would be back "...and ready to do some damage, again."

Name _____

Write your answers on the lines of the pattern.

1. ____

2. ____ ____

3. ____ ____ ____

4. ____ ____ ____ ____

5. ____ ____ ____ ____ ____

6. ____ ____ ____ ____ ____ ____

7. ____ ____ ____ ____ ____ ____ ____

8. ____ ____ ____ ____ ____ ____ ____ ____

9. ____ ____ ____ ____ ____ ____ ____ ____

10. ____ ____ ____ ____ ____ ____ ____ ____ ____

1. She won a silver medal at the Olympics in 199__.

2. The stories agree _____ one thing.

3. She had a good chance to _____the gold medal.

4. She _____ the bicycle without any training.

5. Alison _____ took to cycling as a little girl.

6. Alison arrived in _____ feeling ill.

7. Training was _____.

8. She was _____ by magpies.

9. She began training hard for the 2000 Olympics in _____.

10. In spite of _____, she was still in the race.

Research: Use a map. What large U.S. city lies across the bay from Victoria, British Columbia? What is the name of the island where Victoria is located?

SHANNON **MILLER**

"Queen Yankee"

The Italians fondly called Shannon Miller "Queen Yankee." It was 1990. She was in Italy to compete in gymnastics. It was a major event. Miller won first place in four events. Shannon won the all-around and the vault. She also won the balance beam and the floor exercise.

Shannon was born in Rolla, Missouri in 1977. She began training at the age of five. The uneven bars and the balance beam were her favorite events. In her teens, she was training eight hours a day. The training made her ready for the pressure of the 1992 Olympics. She won five events. She took home two silver and three bronze medals.

In 1996, she and six teammates competed in the Olympics. The team won a gold medal. Shannon won her own gold medal on the beam. After the games, she said, "I want to get a college education. I want to have a career and a family. I want to see what's out there, outside the gym."

In 1999, Shannon received a different kind of gold. The gold was a wedding ring. She married Dr. Chris Phillips. Her six 1996 Olympic teammates were in her wedding party.

Miller has won a total of 16 medals in her career. Seven of them were in the Olympics. Shannon has won more titles in gymnastics than any other U.S. woman. Gymnastics has been part of her life for a long time. In 2000, she stated, "I'm just not ready to give it up."

Name _____

Write the answers on the lines.

1. By what nickname did the Italians call Shannon?_____

2. Why was Shannon in Italy? _____

3. How many events did Miller win in Italy? _____

4. Where was Shannon born? _____

5. How many medals has Shannon won in her career? _____

6. How many of the medals were in the Olympics? _____

7. What kind of gold did Shannon receive in 1999? _____

The following statements are either true or false. Write true or false on the lines.

8. Shannon began training at the age of five. _____

9. In her teens, she was training 10 hours a day._____

10. She won five events in the 1992 Olympics. _____

11. In 1999, she received a gold nose ring. _____

12. Her six Olympic teammates were at her birthday party _____

13. She married Dr. Chris Phillips. _____

14. Shannon has won very few titles in gymnastics. _____

Research: Use an encyclopedia. Find **Friedrich Ludwig Jahn**. He was born August 11,

_____. He was known as the _____ of _____.

Name _____

Playing Smart

"The strongest part of my game is in my head. I play what I feel. I respond to the ball. The rhythm and the timing are much more important to me than power. I never had power. Instead, I had to be smart," Martina remarked.

Before she was two years old, she was holding a tennis racket. Her father had made a small racket for her. She lost the first tournament she ever played. She was only four years old at the time. When she was six, she won!

Martina was born in Czechoslovakia in 1980. She and her mother moved to Switzerland when she was nine. Her mother helped her to develop a creative tennis game. Martina learned to think on the court. Her strong point is her ability to out-think her opponents. To improve her athletic ability, she spent time shadow boxing.

Hingis turned pro at age 14. She played and beat girls who were five and six years older. In her career, she has won five Grand Slams. She

rocketed to first place in women's tennis.

Hingis belongs to a group called Teams to End Poverty. She has traveled to Colombia to visit shelters for street children. The children are taken care of in the shelters. They are helped with their education.

Martina said of her life in tennis, "It's definitely a very exciting career, so far. I've learned a lot and have had many experiences, but it's not over yet."

15

Name _____

Circle the correct answer.

1. Martina was born in _____.
    a. Holland   b. Switzerland   c. Czechoslovakia

2. Her father made her a small _____.
    a. racket   b. swing   c. tennis court

3. Hingis and her mother moved to _____.
    a. Florida   b. Switzerland   c. Germany

4. To improve her athletic ability, she spent time _____.
    a. running   b. cycling   c. shadowboxing

5. Hingis belongs to a group called Teams to _____.
    a. Stop Hunger   b. End Poverty   c. Bring Peace

6. She has traveled to Colombia to visit shelters for _____.
    a. street children   b. sick children   c. the elderly

Write the statements so they are correct.

1. Martina was born in 1985.

    _____

2. Her mother helped her to develop a defensive tennis game.

    _____

3. Hingis played and beat girls two and three years older.

    _____

4. Martina thinks her life in tennis is very dull.

    _____

5. She rocketed to second place in women's tennis.

    _____

Research: Use an encyclopedia. Find **Czechoslovakia**. Draw a picture of the Czech flag and color it.

Name _____

She Lived the Dream

The tower stood 33 feet high. That's about the height of a three-story building. The young woman from Texas stood at the edge of the platform. Laura Wilkinson was the only American in the highboard diving finals. She was in eighth place. Ahead of her were the members of the powerful Chinese team. They were ranked first and second. The Chinese had won titles in four straight Olympics. Each diver would make five dives. These dives would decide who would be the gold medal winner of the 2000 Olympics.

Laura had broken three bones in her foot before the Olympics. She had cracked her foot on the platform while diving. The injury kept her from full training for more than six weeks. She wore a cast and used crutches for a while. She began training again in June for the summer games. She wore a kayak boot between dives to cushion her broken bones. In spite of the setback, Laura kept up her confidence.

After the first dive, Laura was in fifth place behind the Chinese and two Canadians. Her fourth dive was perfect. She advanced to first place. The Chinese teenagers would have to perform without flaws to win. They were unable to match Laura's dive. The gold medal was hers. The last time an American woman had won the 10-meter diving gold medal was in 1964.

Ken Armstrong was her diving coach. After Laura won, he said, "Maybe this is the rebirth of U.S.A. diving. It was time."

Name _____

Write the answers on the lines. Find the answers in the word search.

1. The _____ stands 33 feet high.

2. The young woman from Texas stood at the edge of the _____.

3. Laura was the only _____ in the _____ diving finals.

4. Each diver would make _____ dives.

5. Her fourth dive was _____.

6. They were _____ to match Laura's _____.

7. The _____ medal was hers.

8. Laura had broken three _____ in her foot.

9. She wore a _____ boot to _____ her broken bones.

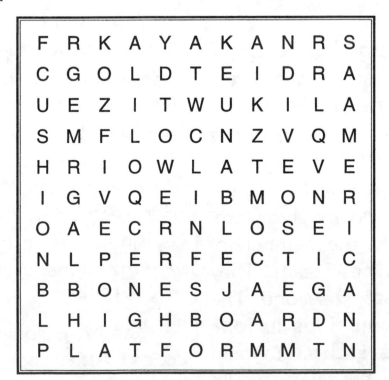

```
F  R  K  A  Y  A  K  A  N  R  S
C  G  O  L  D  T  E  I  D  R  A
U  E  Z  I  T  W  U  K  I  L  A
S  M  F  L  O  C  N  Z  V  Q  M
H  R  I  O  W  L  A  T  E  V  E
I  G  V  Q  E  I  B  M  O  N  R
O  A  E  C  R  N  L  O  S  E  I
N  L  P  E  R  F  E  C  T  I  C
B  B  O  N  E  S  J  A  E  G  A
L  H  I  G  H  B  O  A  R  D  N
P  L  A  T  F  O  R  M  M  T  N
```

Research: Use an encyclopedia. Find **diving**. There are four basic parts of a dive that are judged in competition. Name them.

Name _____

Lisa Leslie is six feet five inches tall. She plays center for the Los Angeles Sparks. The Sparks are a women's pro basketball team.

Lisa was born in 1972 in Los Angeles. Her mother was a long-haul truck driver. Sometimes Lisa and her two sisters would ride with her. "My mom made sure that I was raised properly and was given all the support I needed," she said. Leslie thinks it is important for young people to have role models. Lisa's mother was hers.

The WNBA was started in the U.S. in 1997. Before that, Lisa played in Europe. She also competed in the 1996 Olympics on the U.S. team. They played 52 games leading up to the Olympics. They won them all. Lisa scored 29 points in the final game. The U.S. won the gold medal. In the 2000 Olympics, the women scored a stunning victory over Australia. Again, they took home the gold.

Lisa does more than play basketball. She has taken an interest in helping children. In 1998, she donated a sports complex to her former high school. She heads a group called "Takin' It Inside with Lisa Leslie." This group helps girls to build self-esteem and to set goals.

Lisa is not always serious. There were only minutes left in the last game of the 2000 Olympics. One of the opposing players pulled Lisa's false hair braid out by accident. Lisa laughed. "That's all right. She can have the hair. I've got the gold," she quipped.

Name _____

Complete the sentences with words from the story.

1. Lisa Leslie is six feet _____ _____ tall.

2. She plays _____ for the Los Angeles Sparks.

3. Lisa was born in _____ in Los Angeles.

4. Her mother was a _____ - _____ truck driver.

5. Lisa thinks it is _____ for young people to have

    _____ _____.

6. The WNBA was started in _____.

7. Before that, she played in _____.

8. In the 2000 Olympics, the women scored a stunning victory over

    _____.

9. Lisa does more than play _____.

10. In 1998, she donated a _____ complex to her former

    _____ _____.

11. She heads a group that helps girls to build _____ - _____.

12. Lisa is not always _____.

13. "That's all right. She can have the _____. I've got the

    _____," she quipped.

Research: Use a dictionary. Find **role model**. Write the definition. Who is your role model? Why?

Name _____

The Tigress?

The cause closest to Karrie Webb's heart has little to do with golf. Her coach is wheelchair bound. He has a spinal cord injury. It left him without the use of this arms and legs. Karrie is active in the Christopher Reeve Foundation. The group raises funds for research on spinal cord injuries.

Karrie was born in Australia in 1974. She started playing golf at the age of eight. In her teens, she played as an amateur. In 1994, she turned pro. She qualified for the LPGA in 1996 with a broken bone in her wrist. That year, she was Rookie of the Year. In 1997, Webb won a trophy for having the lowest scoring average.

Her career has been similar to Tiger Woods' career. Meg Mallon is a golfer who has played against Webb. She said, "Karrie has been fabulous. I don't think people talk about her like they talk about Tiger. They talk about Tiger like he is a god and nobody can catch him. I feel like Karrie has played the same way."

By 2000, Webb had 16 career wins. Soon she added more wins to her total. They included two important tours. One was the Australian Ladies' Masters and the other was the U.S. Women's Open. "I still can't believe that I've achieved what I have. It's like I've lived a dream," she said. "It just keeps continuing to happen. I'm just going to go with it for as long as it lasts."

Name _____

Write your answers on the lines of the pattern.

1. _____

2. _____ _____

3. _____ _____ _____

4. _____ _____ _____ _____

5. _____ _____ _____ _____ _____

6. _____ _____ _____ _____ _____ _____

7. _____ _____ _____ _____ _____ _____ _____

8. _____ _____ _____ _____ _____ _____ _____ _____

9. _____ _____ _____ _____ _____ _____ _____ _____ _____

10. _____ _____ _____ _____ _____ _____ _____ _____ _____ _____

1. Karrie was born in Australia in 197__.

2. "I'm just going to _____ with it."

3. She started playing golf at the ___ of eight.

4. She qualified for the ____ in 1996.

5. She had a broken bone in her _____.

6. Her coach has a _____ cord injury.

7. Her career has been _____ to Tiger Woods' career.

8. "Karrie has been _____."

9. Her wins included two _____ tours.

10. One was the _____ Ladies' Masters.

Research: Use a dictionary or an encyclopedia. Find **Great Barrier Reef**. Write a short paragraph describing the reef.

MARION JONES

Running Fast and Jumping Far

Marion Jones had a goal for the 2000 Olympic games. She would compete in five track and field events. She hoped to win a gold medal in each event.

Marion was born in Los Angeles in 1975. She competed against her brother and his friends in races. By the time she was 13, she had outrun all his friends. Then she outran her brother.

In college, Marion played basketball and ran track. Twice, while playing basketball, she broke bones in her foot. She decided to devote her skills to track.

Jones breezed to a win in the 100-meter dash in the 2000 Olympics. Then she took the gold in the 200-meter. The long jump was her most challenging event. She won the bronze. Two team relay races lay ahead of her. Team USA won a gold medal in one relay race. They won a bronze in the other race. When it was all over, Marion's tally was three gold and two bronze medals.

"I wanted to win them all, without a doubt, and I still think it's possible," Jones said. "But I didn't, so I'm not going to dwell on that."

Marion Jones has taken her place in the record books. The last time a woman won three gold medals in track was 1988. Jones is the first woman to win five medals in track in one Olympics. Marion proved she is the best in the world.

Name _____

Circle the correct answer.

1.   Marion Jones had a goal for the 2000 _____.

      a. World Cup   b. Olympics   c. World Record

2.   Marion was born in _____.

      a. Los Angeles   b. Los Alamos   c. Las Vegas

3.   In college, Jones broke bones in her foot while playing _____.

      a. soccer   b. baseball   c. basketball

4.   Jones breezed to a win in the 100-meter _____.

      a. run   b. dash   c. race

5.   Her most challenging event was the _____.

      a. long jump   b. high jump   c. relay race

6.   Jones won two _____.

      a. bronze medals   b. gold medals   c. silver medals

7.   Marion Jones has taken her place in the _____.

      a. record books   b. history books   c. sports magazines

8.   The last time a woman won three gold medals in track was in _____.

      a. 1978   b. 1988   c. 1954

9.   Marion proved she is the best in the _____.

      a. world   b. country   c. Olympics

Research: Use an encyclopedia. Find **Paavo Johannes Nurmi.** Where was he born? What was his sport? How many gold medals did he win in 1924? What was his nickname?

KRISTI **YAMAGUCHI**

Star on Ice

Kristi overcame a severe problem to become a figure skater. In 1971, she was born with a foot that turned in. This caused her leg to be twisted. She wore a cast to straighten her leg and foot. When Kristi was three, her mother put her in a dance class. She also got her started in ice skating lessons. The little girl was not strong. She worked hard to build up her muscles.

Kristi lived with her parents in California. Her hero was Dorothy Hamill. Hamill was a figure skater.

She had won an Olympic gold medal in 1976. Yamaguchi had a doll that looked like Dorothy.

Kristi would get up at 4 a.m. to take lessons at a local rink. Then she went to school. With hard work and natural talent, Kristi began to master ice skating. It became her life.

In 1992, Kristi had a big year. First, she won the U.S. National Championship. Then, she went on to win a gold medal at the Olympics. Next, she became the World Champion. That same year, she turned pro. She placed first in the World Professional Championships.

As a pro, she toured with Stars on Ice. In 2000, she took time from her busy schedule to marry Bret Hedican. He is a hockey player.

Kristi's advice to fans is to "always dream." She should know. She started life as a little girl with a twisted leg. She grew up to be a strong and beautiful woman.

KRISTI **YAMAGUCHI**

Cross out the sentences that DO NOT tell about Kristi Yamaguchi.

Kristi overcame a severe problem to become a figure skater.

She was born in Japan.

Kristi would get up at 4 a.m. to take lessons at a local rink.

Her advice to fans is to "always dream."

In 2000, she retired from ice-skating.

Her hero was Dorothy Hamill.

In 1992, she won an Olympic gold medal.

She married a basketball player.

As a pro, she toured with Stars on Ice.

Her favorite pastime is playing video games.

She grew up to be a strong and beautiful woman.

Write the sentences you have not crossed out in the order they appear in the story.

_____

_____

_____

_____

_____

_____

_____

_____

Research: Use a dictionary. Find **figure skating**. Write the definition.

Name _____

The Dynamic Duo of Tennis

Venus Williams' coach says she needs to improve her serve. Her footwork could be better, too. In spite of these "flaws," she is one of the best players in women's tennis. Venus won the gold medal for singles in the 2000 Olympics. She and Serena, her sister, won the gold for the doubles match. This was the first time a sisters' team had won the doubles.

Venus was born in 1980. Her sister followed 18 months later. They lived in a tough area of Compton, California. Richard, their father, wanted more for his girls. He thought tennis was the game that could give them a better life. He studied books on tennis. He watched tennis videos. He taught his daughters what he learned. The girls learned the game well. In a few years, they needed a professional coach. Richard moved his family to Florida. There, the girls could practice with pros.

Venus joined the pro tennis tour in 1994. Serena hit the pro circuit in 1997. The sisters had always practiced by playing each other. The time came when they met as opponents on the court. In 2000, they faced off at Wimbledon. Venus beat Serena in the semifinals. Venus went on to win the Wimbledon title. It was her first Grand Slam. Serena had won her first Grand Slam a year earlier. They were even.

Venus is the first African-American woman to win the singles title at Wimbledon since 1958.

Name _____

Across

1. This was the first time a sisters team had won the _____.
4. The time came when they met as _____ on the court.
7. Venus is the first _____-American woman to win the singles title at Wimbledon since 1958.
8. The _____ learned the game well.
10. Venus went on to win the _____ title.
12. Venus won the gold medal for _____ in the 2000 Olympics.

Down

2. She and Serena ___ the gold for the doubles match.
3. They needed a _____ coach.
5. They lived in a _____ area.
6. Her ____ followed 18 months later.
9. In spite of the "_____," she is one of the best players in women's tennis.
11. Richard studied books on _____.

Research: Name three well-known duos. They can be from movies, sports, TV, comics, etc.

PG 2 **Across** 1. Aborigine 3. torch 4. talent 6. Olympics 8. hero 10. flame 11. dream **Down** 1. Australian 2. excelled 5. stepdad 7. streaked 9. white **Research:** a blind channel; a usually dry streambed; a backwater forming a stagnant pool; Australia

PG 4 1. the high school coach 2. 16 3. *Answers will vary.* 4. Los Angeles 5. 45 6. Italy; Spain 7. national championships 8. 1997 9. Houston Comets 10. basketball 11. Most Valuable Player **Research:** professional - someone who does something for pay; amateur - someone who does something for pleasure, not for pay; *answers may vary.*

PG 6 1. opinion 2. fact 3. fact 4. opinion 5. opinion 6. fact 7. opinion MEXICAN *Opinions will vary.* **Research:** soccer; Brazil; 1940; New York Cosmos; *Answers will vary.*

PG 8

Research: to join with others in refusing to buy from or deal with a person, nation or business

PG 10 1. false 2. true 3. true 4. true 5. false 6. false 7. false 8. true 9. false 10. true 11. false 12. true FROGS AND DOGS excitement; moved; youngest; gold; history **Research:** Norway; April 8, 1912; figure skating; Norwegian Women's Figure-Skating Title

PG 12 1. 6 2. on 3. win 4. rode 5. Sydor 6. Sydney 7. intense 8. attacked 9. Australia 10. everything **Research:** Seattle, Washington; Vancouver Island

PG 14 1. "Queen Yankee" 2. to compete in gymnastics 3. four 4. Rolla, Missouri 5. 16 6. seven 7. wedding ring 8. true 9. false 10. true 11. false 12. false 13. true 14. false **Research:** 1778; father of gymnastics

PG 16 1. c. Czechoslovakia 2. a. racket 3. b. Switzerland 4. c. shadow boxing 5. b. End Poverty 6. a. street children 1. Martina was born in 1980. 2. Her mother helped her to develop a creative tennis game. 3. Hingis played and beat girls five and six years older. 4. Martina thinks her life in tennis is very exciting. 5. She rocketed to first place in women's tennis.

Research:

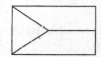

blue triangle, white top bar, red bottom bar

PG 18 1. tower 2. platform 3. American; highboard 4. five 5. perfect 6. unable; dive 7. gold 8. bones 9. kayak; cushion

```
F R K A Y A K A N R S
C G O L D T E I D R A
U E Z I T W U K I L A
S M F L O C N Z V Q M
H R I O W L A T E V E
I G V Q E I B M O N R
O A E C R N L O S E I
N L P E R F E C T I C
B B O N E S J A E G A
L H I G H B O A R D N
P L A T F O R M M T N
```

Research: the run; the takeoff; the execution; the entry into the water

PG 20 1. five inches 2. center 3. 1972 4. long-haul 5. important; role models 6. 1997 7. Europe 8. Australia 9. basketball 10. sports; high school 11. self-esteem 12. serious 13. hair; gold **Research:** a person who is inspiring in some role or position and so serves as a model for others; *Answers will vary.*

PG 22 1. 4 2. go 3. age 4. LPGA 5. wrist 6. spinal 7. similar 8. fabulous 9. important 10. Australian **Research:** coral reef; 1250 miles long; in Coral Sea off the northeast coast of Queensland, Australia

PG 24 1. b. Olympics 2. a. Los Angeles 3. c. basketball 4. b. dash 5. a. long jump 6. a. bronze medals 7. a. record books 8. b. 1988 9. a. world **Research:** Finland; long-distance running; five; The Flying Finn

PG 26 **Cross out:** She was born in Japan. In 2000, she retired from ice-skating. She married a basketball player. Her favorite pastime is playing video games. **Write:** Kristi overcame a severe problem to become a figure skater. Her hero was Dorothy Hamill. Kristi would get up at 4 a.m. to take lessons at a local rink. In 1992, she won an Olympic gold medal. As a pro, she toured with Stars on Ice. Her advice to fans is to "always dream." She grew up to be a strong and beautiful woman. **Research:** ice skating in which the performer traces various detailed figures on the ice

PG 28 **Across** 1. doubles 4. opponents 7. African 8. girls 10. Wimbledon 12. singles **Down** 2. won 3. professional 5. tough 6. sister 9. flaws 11. tennis **Research:** *Answers will vary.*

Need more practice? Try these other books from . . .

◆◆◆◆ REMEDIA PUBLICATIONS ◆◆◆◆

Daily Comprehension—*Grades 5–12/Rdg. Level 3–4*
September .... Item Number REM 1101
October .... Item Number REM 1102
November .... Item Number REM 1103
December .... Item Number REM 1104
January .... Item Number REM 1105
February .... Item Number REM 1107
March .... Item Number REM 1108
April .... Item Number REM 1109
May .... Item Number REM 1110

Reading for Details—*Grades 4–8*
Rdg. Level 3 .... Item Number REM 489A
Rdg. Level 4 .... Item Number REM 489B

Comparing—*Grades 5–8/Rdg. Level 3–4*............................ Item Number REM 490

Specific Skills Series—*Grades 6–12/Rdg. Level 3*
Locating Information .... Item Number REM 4001
Fact and Opinion .... Item Number REM 4002
Making Inferences .... Item Number REM 4003

Read and Remember—*Grades 4–8*
Rdg. Level 3–4 .... Item Number REM 496A
Rdg. Level 3–4 .... Item Number REM 496B

Famous People/Amazing Facts—*Grades 4–8/Rdg. Level 2.0–4.5*
Famous People, Places, and Events .... Item Number REM 1115A
Amazing Facts .... Item Number REM 1114A

＊Comprehension Quickies—*Grades 4–8*
Rdg. Level 2 .... Item Number REM 440
Rdg. Level 3 .... Item Number REM 441

＊Wonder Stories—*Grades 4–8*
Rdg. Level 2 .... Item Number REM 467
Rdg. Level 5 .... Item Number REM 470

＊Reading to Learn Series—*Grades 4–12/Rdg. Level 3–4*
Presidents .... Item Number REM 418
Inventors .... Item Number REM 419
Strange Tales .... Item Number REM 437

＊Labeling for Comprehension
Rdg. Level 3 .... Item Number REM 448
Rdg. Level 4 .... Item Number REM 449

Finding the Main Idea—*Grades 4–8/Rdg. Level 4*............. Item Number REM 484

＊Cloze Procedure—*Grades 4–8*
Rdg. Level 2 .... Item Number REM 412
Rdg. Level 3 .... Item Number REM 413

RPP9004
*More titles in this series are available.

. . . and much more!